HUGS & KISSES

HUGS & KISSES

by Bruce Davis, Ph.D. and Genny Wright

Illustrated by Genny Wright

Workman Publishing Company, New York

Library of Congress Cataloging in Publication Data

Davis, Bruce, 1950-
  Hugs & kisses.

  SUMMARY: Explains the importance of being kind
to yourself and others.
  1. Love. 2. Self-acceptance. 3. Interpersonal
relations. [1. Love. 2. Self-acceptance.
3. Interpersonal relations] I. Wright, Genny, joint
author. II. Title.
BF575.L8D35   158'.2   77-5283
ISBN: 0-89480-008-6 cloth
ISBN: 0-89480-106-6 paper

Jacket design by Paul Hanson
Book design by Barbara Bedick

Workman Publishing Company, Inc.
708 Broadway
New York, New York 10003

Manufactured in the United States of America
First printing September 1977
25 24 23 22 21 20 19 18

We wish to thank
our mothers and fathers
who first shared with us
hugs and kisses;
and each other
for the love which
made this book possible.

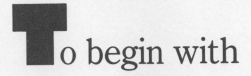

To begin with

The most
important thing
to know is that you
deserve
lots and lots
of hugs and kisses.

Did you hear that?

You deserve lots and lots of hugs and kisses.

Because you
are the only
you there is,
and you're special!

You believe in you
and know that you
deserve hugs and
kisses —
lots of them.

Do I deserve a kiss?

I do.
I do.
I do!

But what *is* a kiss?

Some people think
that a kiss is
something you do
with your lips.

But a kiss is really
something you do
to make you
and someone else
feel better.

Anything you do
that feels good
can be a kiss.

Sometimes you do
not use your mouth
at all, but instead you
use your toes to kiss.

On a hot summer day
there is the
ice cream kiss.

And on a cold
winter day
there is the
blanket kiss
to keep you both
warm.

Sometimes you just use your little finger to kiss a hurt.

Sometimes you print
on a sheet of paper
   "I LIKE YOU"
and give it to a friend.

This, too, is really
just another way
to kiss.

Sending a note
can be a special
way to kiss
a shy friend.

Being brave enough
to open a door
and say "hello"
may be a way to
kiss an angry friend.

A sour friend may be
the hardest to
sweeten,
because something is
upset inside.

Sharing your only
candy bar may be
the secret.

For a friend
who is sick
there is the
intravenous kiss.

This is when
a kiss enters
the blood stream
and rushes to
wherever it is
most needed.

Kisses can be as long, big, and noisy

or as short, small,
and quiet
as you and your friend
want them to be.

Sometimes a flying kiss
is the best thing to do.

And sometimes only a
flying wet kiss will
share your feeling.

There is always the angel kiss.

Angel kisses can be
made anytime,
anywhere.
Just think of your most
special invisible friend
and know that he or
she is
kissing you...
and kiss back.

If you want
you can kiss God.

Kissing sunsets, trees,
a little girl's knee;

kissing Mommy
and Daddy,
your favorite toy;
kissing everything you
normally kiss or
never kiss
are all different ways
of kissing God.

And if you get tired
of kisses,
you can say
    "No!"
whenever you want.

NO!

Kisses, like gifts,
are for when
you feel like giving
and receiving.

But what about hugs?

Hugs, like kisses, can be shared with much more than just people.

You can hug your
favorite
stuffed animal,
imaginary friend,
or pet lizard.

You can hug a flower,
but you must hug
gently.

There is the back to back hug.

There is the
reluctant hug.

There is the short
distance hug
where you hug elbows,
fingers, ankles
anything close to you.

When a friend is far away, there is the long distance hug.

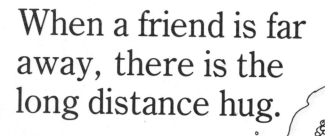

Hug anything dear
to you,
wish it to your friend,
and feel your friend
hugging you too!

And if no hug can
be found,
stand in front of
a mirror
and look at the most
wonderful person
in the world
and hug yourself!

With hugs and kisses, the more love you give yourself, the more love you have for others.

There are hugging and
kissing exercises,
where you can
hug and kiss
anyplace,
anytime,

and your hugs and
kisses will
get better and better.

"But I want a hug and a kiss from you!"

You can hug and kiss
with all your friends
in a park,

or with someone
special
in your own secret
spot.

Hugs and kisses can be
sharing the smallest
thought

or coming together for
one big squeeze.

Hugs and kisses is
discovering your heart.

and exploring all that
you deserve.

The deeper you look inside, the more you find to love and share.

Hugs and kisses is trusting the love inside you.